Double Trouble Vol. III

Ah but I may as well
try and catch the wind

Donovan Leitch
(from the song "Catch the Wind")

Other Collabs
by Matthew Jose and Candice James

Double Trouble Volume I - poems from the edge
Double Trouble Volume II - deviate the levitate

Double Trouble Vol. III

Poemetrics

by

**Matthew Jose
&
Candice James**

720 Sixth Street, Unit #5,
New Westminster, BC Canada
V3L3C5

Title: Double Trouble Vol. III
Authors: Matthew Jose and Candice James
Publisher: Silver Bow Publishing
Cover: 'Fish Out of Water / I Don't Want To Swim Without You Baby'
 Painting © Candice James
Layout and editing: Candice James

All rights reserved including the right to reproduce or translate this book or any portions thereof, in any form without the permission of the publisher. Except for the use of short passages for review purposes, no part of this book may be reproduced, in part or in whole, or transmitted in any form or by any means, electronically or mechanically, including photocopying, recording, or any information or storage retrieval system without prior permission in writing from the publisher or a license from the Canadian Copyright Collective Agency (Access Copyright). Copyright to all individual poems remains with the author.
© Silver Bow Publishing 2021

97817740301674 Print
97817740301681 epub

Library and Archives Canada Cataloguing in Publication

Title: Double trouble. Vol. III : poemetrics / by Matthew Jose & Candice James.
Names: Jose, Matthew, 1976- author. | James, Candice, 1948- author.
Identifiers: Canadiana (print) 20210323264 | Canadiana (ebook) 20210323302 | ISBN 9781774031674
   (softcover) | ISBN 9781774031681 (EPUB)
Classification: LCC PS3610.O75 D695 2022 | DDC 811/.6—dc23

"I found it!
Sweet Jesus I found the missing ink stain!
The one that's been hiding all the words I never said."

(excerpt from 'The Gathering')

~ Matthew Jose & Candice James

Double Trouble Vol. III

Contents

Watered-Down Drinks ... 9
Ferry Boats ... 11
Hangover ... 13
Panhandling and Handling Pans ... 15
The Gathering ... 17
Golden Spoons and Satin Shirts ... 20
Right, Write and Egypt ... 21
The Lines ... 23
Poemetrics... 25
Yin and Yang ... 27
Threshold ... 29
Imagine That ... 30
Impressive Isn't It ... 32
Let's Go. Shall We? ... 34
Long Before. Long After ... 36
Marvelous Fulfillments ... 37
Not Sorry ... 39
Synaptic Synching ... 41
Happy Corpse ... 43
Relenting Hope ... 44
Revelations Round About Midnight ... 46
Ruminating on Nothing ... 48
Scheme of Things ... 50
Some Ancient Fellow ... 52
Some Footprints ... 53
Something Like ... 54
Sometimes It Happens ... 55
Only an Ism Away ... 57
The Cold Nights of Albuquerque ... 59
The Gods Are Not Crazy ... 61
The Unison of Opposites ... 62
Thick in the Middle ... 64
Title ... 65
Truth of Consequences ... 67
Vague and Prickly ... 70
When the Wind Drops ... 72

Double Trouble Vol. III

What's Left? ... 74
What Then? ...75

Author Profile ... 76

Watered-Down Drinks

Pardon me, but you're sitting in my seat.
I threw Earth time into Evidarian suspension.
I've been gone two light years. Just an eye-blink to you,
and I'm not sure what's happening right now,
but I know this is my seat and I was just gone for a second
as I just wanted to see if that bearded guy over there
(due double north from where I'm sitting)
at the other side of the long neck bar
is really sitting with his back to the wall also.
I ambled on over and took a peek.
Sure enough, he was. I like that.
Already I respect him.

And now the pondering begins.
I wonder what genetic interdimensional idiosyncrasy
makes us both orient ourselves in that same way.
I had asked around about him. I was curious yellow.
Rather strange since I was wearing black, green, red and blue.
After many mini-interviews, the main take-away was this:
A lot of people said they thought his seating choices
were the most admirable thing about him.
Struck me as very odd, Cat had my tongue.
So I shuffled off to due double south.
From whence I came once I got back to Earth.

Back at my table, the waitress returns with our drinks.
She carries them as if they are unreal blurry notions
that got carried away in her mind
and carried over somehow into my realm of existence.

Then suddenly just like that,
I think back to my kindred 'back to the wall' seat patron.
It seemed like he had his own henchmen.
One on either side of him.
Maybe they were from Evidaris too. Incognito.
I like that too. In a certain trenchmen way.

Ok, enough about the patron ... back to the drinks.
Turns out the bartender is a low-down dirty rat
and a goddamn crook too. Pardon my Cagney.
How can a drink taste watered-down
when we ordered doubles?

Just as I'm about to beckon the manager
for a Howard Stern Hollywood word or two about *"the help"*,
I see, stumbling into the place, some classic movie escapees;
a bunch of 18th century cowboy intellectuals.

They meander down all the way
to the dark end of the time-warped bar.
It's one of those mahogany gold moments.

Where did that movement even originate?
Not the movement to the dark end of the bar.
I mean the 18th century cowboy intellectual movement.
Was it an enlightenment thing?
Was it just my imagination?
Or ... holy faulty water taps Batman ...
was it those dastardly watered-down drinks!

Ferry Boats

I've had the wind taken out of me
jumping off swimming pool diving boards
but I've never lost a couple of 6 rounders
and I've never been on a ferry boat.
But that's ok.

> Sometimes something is heard
> when nothing has even been said.

Yeah the wind has been taken out of my sails
plenty of times over plenty of tears
and plenty of years.
And the fact I've never been on a ferry boat
doesn't even bother me anymore.
I've never been a good swimmer
so the shore was more my speed.

> Sometimes something is found
> when nothing has even been lost.

The things we long for
might have proven to be very detrimental
had we actually gotten them.
Divine intervention? Mebbee.
Call it whatever you want to call it.

> Sometimes something is granted
> when nothing has even been wished for.

Stranger things than this happen every moment.
That we may have failed to notice or recognize.
And that's ok.

> Sometimes something is recognized
> when nothing has even been noticed.

The nice thing, when you really think about it,
is that nothing matters now and really never has.

Nothing really matters
Nothing really matters to me.
But still ... I often think about ferry boats.

Hangover

I see bedsheets with "the night before" type of ruffles
but nobody is in the room except the ghost chasing me.
I had come over to see her once before,
but this time I arrived unannounced and alone
or so I thought until I glanced into the mirror
and saw him again, hazy, wisping in and out..

Looking around her room I notice all the shades are drawn.
That's good. Sunshine can be so oppressive at times.
9:00 in the morning on a Saturday and my ghost is awake.
The mailman comes by. We chat it up for a minute.
He has the commanding voice of a cool dude
like one of the great drunk philosophers of the past,
not sure who, but def one of them.

I decide to leave and get on with my day.
No sense waiting for a bus that may never come.

The neighborhood is littered with broken-down cars.
Reminds me of broken-down dives I've lived in
Huck sacks where some of the best parts of me died.
Where local zoot-suiters were my only allies.
Oh yeah, and the cockroaches of my nights.
How they loved to join me when the lights went out.
Those were the days, man. Not.

So I'm walkin' along like a hungover philosopher
philosophizing the night we had the week before.
The night that was our first night ... last night?
The night that was such a night ... living magic.
And those kind of starts usually end up badly for me.

With women it's always like a hangover for me.
You don't cure a hangover.
You just wait for the next drink to fix it.

Was she that next drink for me? Or just the last bitters
hanging over from the night before still hanging onto me.

Times like this when I think too much
are always the root of the hangover ...
hangin' in, hangin' on, hangin' out
in all the wrong mindsets I've inherited.
The "do it again" demons I can't seem to silence.

Walking, knowingly, into the oppressive sun
I realize, you can't cure a heartache.
You just have to wait for the next kiss to fix it.

Panhandling and Handling Pans

Sometimes it looks like every day common sense
isn't a part of the fundamental notions anymore.
I see this as I listen intently to the sound of somebody
carpentering somewhere off in the distance.
I wonder if that is an extraordinarily enjoyable occupation.
Listening intently I mean.
I feel like it would help with presenting a satisfactory answer.
Listening intently I mean.

Do you think the panhandlers
at the exit on ramps and off ramps
have a plan in mind or if their just pandering time?
mishandling time in manhandling time.
I would like to think there is a plan.
but to some people "one day at a time" really means that.
It's like the monks and the skid row dwellers
are the only ones that can really get to know that.
Right? Wrong? A poem? A song?
Git along little dogie get along.

The rest of us are regular and clocklike.
In a mechanical way but not in a bad way.
More like it's a natural thing, after all, kind of way.

If we act at once and instantaneously
would we gain more or would we lose ourselves
to that other self that's always hiding in the shadows
just putting in time and waiting ...waiting.?

Exiting off the on ramp of my freewheeling mind
I think I'm going to spring for a granite pan
and park myself on the off ramp
and just handle it as many ways as I can.
And when I really get good at it, I'll buy another two pans
and I'll learn how to juggle them
and I'll become the prince of the panhandlers,

And my off ramp will be lined up for miles
just so they can see me juggle those heavy granite pans.
Three circling around in the air under the guidance
of my nimble thimble calloused hands, and always,
always there is one mother of a shiny granite pan
gleaming on the ground gathering coins
at break-neck, throttle down, get it on speed.

One time, I time travelled back to the 60s
and did a guest shot on the Ed Sullivan show
It was a *REALLY BIG SHEW* for sure
and the encores were so stupendous
that the last 3 acts didn't get a chance to go on.
I closed the REALLY BIG SHEW with a high falutin' kick
and really brought the house down.

Aaah yes, but that was then, and this is now.
And I'm just panhandling my life away
in a whirlwind of granite dreams.
Polishing them to diamonds
in the eternal sunshine of my mind.

Eat your heart out juggler wannabees.
Oh yeah, and I don't give no lessons.
If you want it, you gotta learn it the hard way.
There ain't no easy roads man ... ain't no easy roads.
I gotta stand up and testify to that!
Like "amen" in the church.

The Gathering

Suppose at this very instant
each of us were open to all possibilities.

Suppose at this very second
you saw yourself waking up in a diner
at the end of the highway in my universe
where the signpost is constantly changing names.

Suppose at this very moment
Hunter S. Thompson was sitting in the diner booth
with sensei and me.

Suppose for a milli-second you're an interdimensional ghost
and you're sitting with us hanging on our every word
extra-sensorily eavesdropping, so to speak.

We know you're right here with us,
a singular plurality of questionable depth.
We sense you but can't structure you into form
so we just continue on as if you're not here.

Time immemorial just keeps on truckin' down the lost highway
and wow! Look at that! Aldous Huxley just walked in.
I beckon him come and sit, he accepts, slides on into the seat
with true finesse and the greatest of ease
like the daring young man on the flying trapeze.
Yes! Perfect, I think. What a fearsome foursome, I think.
Word whips we are. Let the circus begin!

Sensei is sipping green tea and picking at a blueberry pie
looking to find one of the 24 bluebirds hiding inside it.
Hunter is sipping black coffee and Jack Daniels sour mash
and picking incessantly at his fingernails
looking for that renegade ink stain that got away.
Aldous is sipping some sort of aphrodisiac and espousing
why it's good for us when we suffer in silence.

I'm sipping a neon, nuclear mimosa and thinking ...
Aldous might be on to something.

Suddenly Hunter jumps up screaming "I found it!
Sweet Jesus I found the missing ink stain!
The one that's been hiding all the words I never said."

Aldous knows those words are worth their weight in gold,
And by God, he wants them. Has to have them.
He lunges at Hunter as sensei and I sit there agog.

Alas, it isn't to be. Roy Rogers gallops in on his weary,
overworked, and very underpaid, palomino, Trigger.
He jumps from his saddle, grabs a quick scotch and soda.
Downs it like a thirsty high-plains drifter,
walks up to Aldous and Hunter, draws his six-guns and drawls,
'Easy boys. I think you word-whackers got somethin' that's mine,
And if it ain't mine, well ... it will be in a few minutes.
Hand it over you over-the-hill washed- out wannabee heroes.'

That proves too much for our interdimensional ghost.
He reveals himself and we are shocked silly Willie!
It's Long John Baldry swingin' his guitar like a quill,
singin' his heart out in deerskin cut time
and adamantly swearing all the blue ink stains are his.
Tut tut ... typical displaced Englishman blues singer.

Anyhow, long story short. The wife shows up.
Dale Evans saunters in snapping her wifely whip
and whips both Roy and Trigger into shape right quick.
They leave. The interdimensional ghost settles down.
John Baldrey is nowhere to be seen. Stole Hunter's ink stains.
Disappeared into the peeling wallpaper
and Hunter is dashing around like a mad thing
trying to pick up on Baldry's trail. Needs those ink stains.
Has to get those words he never said back.
Aldous is just happy the melee is over.
He picks up his drink and sips it intermittently
between shallow breaths and deep sighs of relief.

And sensei and I? We remain calm as usual,
continue pulling on our drinks
and pull out our pens to write this poem
to give to you ...
and the world.

Nothin' left to say,
so semi-sayonara baby faces
and ta-ta for now.

Golden Spoons and Satin Shirts

Tin Horn lawmen and silver spurs janglin'
never did turn my crank.
Gruff unshaven outlaws with sawed off shotguns
were always more my style.

I once knew a Me-hi-can bandido
who had gold bullets in his gun belt
and always had a choke hold on his colt 45.
This guy was a real bad ass dude
and that in itself was kind of rare
because he grew up in the lap of luxury
in a Mexican palace. His daddio was the governor
and he was related to the real-life Zorro.
     swish, swish, swish.

He said he used to dress for breakfast
in a white satin shirt and black leather pants,
eat his porridge with a golden spoon,
wipe his mouth with a velvet napkin
and life was good and kept going on ...
and on and on.

When I saw him lying dead in the street,
white satin shirt splotched crimson with blood,
a golden spoon in his mouth
and silver bullets in his chest,
I realized then:
White satin shirts can't deflect death.
Golden spoons often choke.
And life goes on and on ...
until it doesn't.

Right, Write and Egypt

When I'm wrong, I'm wrong.
And even though I'm the last to admit it. I do admit it.

But supposing I'm right. What then?
You think that would mean it's time to celebrate?
On the contrary. It would simply mean a nod at that moment.
Short lived and soon forgotten.
I've seen right change to wrong in time.
and right change to left in mime.
I'm sitting here trying, for the life of me,
to think of something that doesn't change in time.

It couldn't be love, right? Or could it?
I've left some women idling at the altar.
and some women have left me standing there stood up.
I've seen love fly out the window
and close the door in the same space and time exactly.
Love is a super power ... can be right or wrong.
So I guess love is out of the discussion.

It couldn't be hate, right? Or could it?
I've seen enemies become friends.
And I've seen friends become enemies.
And then there's those politically incorrect
mugwump bastards known as frenemies.
Those tap-dancing, line-crossing convenient quitters.
We all know at least one of them thar fence sitters.
Don't we? You bet we do!
The real-life slump hitters always striking out
but somehow never losing or being ejected from the game.
And I've seen some astonishing feats of forgiveness.
So I guess hate is out too. At least sometimes.
May I whisper it? ... *'Those times few and far between.'*

I once heard a twinkie will last forever
if you put it on a shelf and forget about it.

So I'm going to grab one today
and hide it away somewhere in the house.
In the name of science.
And curiosity.

But supposing I was to make my own papyrus.
Could I ever possibly make it as durable
as the sheets of Egyptian origin?
I remember ruminating on this once.
So much so it started to concern me.
I reckoned there was only one thing I could do at that point.
So I made my own papyrus. Right there in my kitchenette.
And when it was finished, I mailed it to the Egyptian embassy
with the hopes of an official opinion of its quality.
I still haven't heard back from anyone
so I'm assuming they are still considering my paper's rank
amongst all other contenders. If there are any.
Maybe there isn't and I'll be tops by default. Not my fault.
That was 6 years ago and nary a word yet.
They must really take this kind of thing seriously.

So, while I'm waiting ever so patiently for an answer
I have been spending my time making a stylish stylus.
I am crafting it out of heavy-duty plastic straws
that I stole from the local McDonalds (They can afford it).
My only worry now is that I'll hear back from Egypt
before my zircon engraved straw stylus is finished.
I just don't want these Egyptian endeavors
I've put my blood, sweat and tears into
to be a write-off ...if you know what I mean ...
and I'll bet you do jellybean. I'll bet you do!

The Lines

The secret to the thing is in the line.
But it's also in the enjoyment and the energy of the line.
In the curvature of the edge and the sharpness of the corner
and the in between simplicity that runs rampant if allowed.
I get high'n love lyin' like a lion in these lines.
I feel like a letter. I feel like a vowel.
Like Marilyn Monroe and Simon Cowell.
Sometimes I gong out and throw in the towel.
But no matter the cost I never call foul.

I feel like a word. I just want to howl ... at the moon.
The moon that's married to that looker 'honey'.
If you're lucky you might see them in June.
Or is that a harvest moon? Or a spice worm in Dune
humping up and down in and out of the sand
and doing it straight up in a desert sand line.
A fine line of heavy sand immovable by hurricanes.
A line to hold the line and hold the fort
for the driver of the spice worm vehicle ...
The sandman chasing Dwight Yoakum and Lady Gaga.
and I don't mean that midnight dude
that drops gritty shit in your eyes to make you sleep.
No this poem-story just isn't that deep,
but it is all about the meaningful lines.
The fine, fine, super fine lines. The specialty lines.
I feel at home there. I feel good there.
Especially when I'm coloring between them.
So I lift a glass of Crayola wax wine... Cheers
And here's to feeling good all the time.

What does it mean again?
When someone says a rose is a rose is a rose?
It depends on how you read it
and it depends on your vantage point when you read it.
That's my whole point. Where the lines meet at angles.
That type of line traveling light and able to stay straight

holds the binary essential lessons we need to understand
to understand ourselves and the lines we are.
I tried to get it. I really did but I couldn't ingest it.
couldn't digest it, couldn't divest it.

So I traveled across many different dimensions,
gathering up multi-cultural zeros and ones
seeking the answers to the questions I lost years ago
in some distant water-logged booze can.
I started to read something or other
from a twisted sister or a broken brother
but then I remembered I'm an only child and an orphan too.
So who were these irrelevant imposters trying to be relatives?
Where did they come from and better yet... Why me?
It was almost too much to keep thinking about
so I fell asleep because I had to in order to remain sane.

When I woke up someone was talking to me, asking me
'Would you prefer the straight stuff instead
or do you want to stick with that rot-gut Crayola wax wine?
I decided to leave the Crayola daze behind me.
It was time to grow up. Graduate into adulthood.

I lifted my Foster Grant's, stared into the sun,
lifted my tumbler and swigged down the straight stuff,
made a bee-line for the closest straight line.

In the curvature of the edge
and the sharpness of the corner
I laid down in the movement of linear time
moving inside the telephone lines
attached to the static in my minds.

I have two of them, you know.
One for here and one for there
and none for anywhere.

How do I know?
The lines told me so.

Poemetrics

Alrighty then.... What? No. Don't call me Jim or Ace.
Don't get it? You can *'Ventura'* guess if you *'Carey'* to. No?
So again, alrighty then ... today's subject is POEMETRICS!

It's poems yes. It's poetry yes.
It's short poem stories. It's short poetic stories.
Sort of flash poems, but not just flash poems,
But short story poems of the 7th kind.
I say the 7th kind because they're more than 6, less than 8
and weren't meant to be discovered or uncovered yet,
but here they are in living scatters of breath.
In your face poeshtories, phonetically: po-e-shtories ...
Stands for (*poem short stories*).
Nothing in common but can rhyme with suppositories.
Yeah, yeah, I know ... what a crappy comparison.

Anyhow, I confess I digress. What a mess
but I am the sanitation man and I'm here to clean this mess up
or at the very least, clear it up.

Ya pick up the stylus Cyrus and you gear up the mind
and you let the good times roll baby.
Like an ace in the hole
Let 'em walk. Let 'em stroll.
Let 'em rip. Let 'em roll
right off the synapses onto the thin tree remnants.
You got it Bobbit...
Paper ... we call it paper ... paper by the reams.
Coffees by the creams, visions by the dreams.
Consarn it... my gramps used to say that a lot.
Again... I digress, so now back to the poemetrics.

These creative endeavors of the 7th kind
are really a much-needed fresh slap in the face
from the semi-playful backhand of the new kid on the block
the gregarious grandstand of a new candidate.

Elect yourself to be a pioneer of this new poetry movement.
POEMETRICS: Calisthenics of the subconscious mind.
Prosthetics of the sentence missing structured words.
Robotics of the 27th kind. They are the missing link
now simulating into the spaces between synapses
to make us humanetrics that know more ... show more.
Paramours to adore before the restore of more.
Denizens of the deep knowing what to toss or keep.
Astronauts of the new wordified domain
Only accessible to the stoically sane.
You get what I mean Jellybean??

I'm stating my case loud, strong and CLEAR:
I'm standing tall and saying: HEAR! HEAR!

POEMETRICS man! That's where it's at.
Can't find it? It's the 27th letter of the alphabet.
The Evidarian alphabet which is accessible to all.
Just close your eyes and chant phonetically with fervor:
PO EH MEH TRIX ... PO EH MEH TRIX ... 27 times.
And your mind will open to the new real deal
and your creative force will be set free
to compose the happy crazy scribblings
so often avoided by your siblings.
Be a happy crazy intellectual meanderer
wandering the hills of poesy personified.

POEMETRICS man! That's where it is.
Find it man... ya just gotta find it!!

Try it ... you'll love it.

Yin and Yang

Have you ever seen a thing that doesn't necessarily fit our world?
Almost like an archaic reference couched in a foreign language.
So much can happen in 17 syllables: NOTE:
(in the background Capt. Picard greets his nemesis, "Hi Q")
Not 'Hello Q'. Not 'What's up Q'. Just simply "Hi Q"
The contempt, only slightly veiled in his voice, is always evident.
Have you ever noticed that? Data did.

The old stories and classic movies
always used to highlight the critical points.
Have you ever noticed that?
It's very hard to replicate the conversational discourses
of 2 very great masters.
Like trying to get Rambo to behave at a Judy Dench tea party.
Both attempting to find a common battleground
to exchange mild pleasantries. Never succeeds.
Judy always has her pinky bent
in aristocratic *'snobs are careless'* display.
Stallone's pinky was broken, and it healed bent
so he looks like he's being polite ... but it's just a ruse.
Sort of like asking Judi and Syl to host and judge
Garth Reynolds and Joe Wright as competition features
freestylin' slam poems at the Copa Cabana. Never works.
The orchestra always escalates and drowns out the poetry.
Have you ever noticed that? Barry Manilow did.

Have you ever read a poem that had so many references to poetry
before that time that it felt like you were reading T.S. Elliot?
In fact, by the time you finished reading it
you weren't even sure where you were or who you were.
References can really screw you up directionally.
Especially if you're a left/right, up/down person
and not a North/South, East/West kinda guy.
You just get messed up and squares run in circles.
And try as you may, you're goin' nowhere fast.
Ever noticed that? The compass and the map did.

Have you ever been accused of being death obsessed?
Almost judged solely on a fascination with the macabre.
Like when you show up at a posh costume party.
You in a suit (Harold). Her in old make-up & balding wig (Maude).
And all your friends wonder why you're so depressed
when you find out you didn't win. Judged wrongly.
Ever notice that? Chidiock Tichborne did.

And because of that wrong judge
have you ever tried to explain to someone
that there is so much at stake with each breath?
You can't expound too much on that lesson.
Chidi tried to, but alas the papers were already graded
and school was out forever.

We all have things that don't fit with our narrative.
We're all conversationalists in ongoing discourse.
We're all living poems recited as we speak.
We're all death obsessed but few will admit it.
We're all judges and all of us judged.
We're all born to die and must die to be born.

We all have our points of departure pre-destined.
Don't we?
And we all have our Earth arrivals written in blood.
Don't we?
We are all yin, and we are all yang
nestled forever between birth and death.
Yes, we are.

Threshold

I can always tell when I've passed my threshold.
Traveling with the greats of old will do that to a poet.
Can you imagine having a regular correspondence
with Seneca? Or Li Po?
Think on that for a little while. Blow your mind buds.
It's on the house man.

I can always tell when someone is carrying a stoic philosophy
on the hip or in their back pocket and sporting a sour face.
I always thought that that stuff was supposed to be enjoyable.
Is that too near-absolute and deranged for some?
Am I wrong? Mebbee so. Mebbee not.

But that's just the beginning of what I've always thought.
There's the obvious denial of the singularity of the thing.
And there's that whole interconnectedness angle too.
These are the thoughts never far from my mind.

I can always tell when a poet wants to put it
within the reach of everybody.
They will ask things like,
"What scene are you digging into right now?"
Or something like,
"When was the last time you took notes
while listening to an Alan Watts lecture?"

When they don't answer and gawk at me funny
with that 'who's this weirdo' expression on their face,
it's then that I know the importance of knowing …
when I've passed my threshold.

Imagine That

There are so many shades of discolored fingernails
and just as many discolored hearts.
And there may be a good reason for the discoloration.
Or it may be a reflection of a tarnished psyche.
Or maybe it's the other brother of immaculate things.
Or the separation of siblings out of synch.
Imagine how that must feel.

Once there were old stories coloring the days of our youth.
Shared hand-me-down stories not meant for publication.
Meant more for fun and pleasure and family bonding.
Crayons waxing technicolor hours to a shine.
Then seeing them crushed in the weight of the dark.
Imagine how that felt.

There's a kind of homeopathy to the whole thing.
A squared science circling the perimeter of the past.
A full circle, ashes to ashes and dust to dust kind of vibe.
A cycling boomerang there and back, then there again
but Rolf's boomerang didn't come back. I stole it.
Imagine how he felt as he was searching all over the place.
Just searching and turning blue in the face.

Imagine reaching out with all your might to grab something
but there's nothing to catch hold of.
Just a bunch of thin chattering air in the thick of it.
Imagine trying to catch a frog by the tail.
Or pin a tail on a tadpole in a rigged never-win game.
Imagine being blinded by a light that strobes the wrong way,
And seems to have it in for only you.
Imagine how that would feel.

Imagine doing choreographed summersault steps
across a water world moving dance floor
to a famous Irving Berlin score.
with the vivacious Flummerfelt sisters we all adore.

They were the original dance hall dollies.
American pioneers those Maureens and Mollies.
They were headed for the posh halls of Manhattan.
One had a date with the Lord Mountbatten
but their stagecoach was robbed, and they were abducted:
To sing and dance in the wild west saloons.
To live and die in the company of goons,
being pushed through those creaky swinging doors.
Standing in a receiving line of tawdry takers.
Wishing to God they had been born Quakers.
Imagine how that felt.

I imagine I might have an idea of how they felt:
If I sailed with the dastardly Captain Ahab
across the seven seas walking the plank in ripped dungarees.
I might hook onto an inkling of insight.

If I served as Hitler's Nazi hit man
and was castrated for carrying out his plans.
then I might have an empty bag of understanding.

If I fought the good fight with all my might
and was crucified for my second sight
I might be able to nail it.

If I walked ever so humbly
through the mosques of Timbuktu
and tripped on an invisible guide-wire of gauze
that brought the walls tumbling down.
Then, I imagine I might have the smallest idea.
of how they felt, but alas, alack,
I'm pretty hard-headed, so maybe not.

Time to ditch the daydreams ... BUT
I'm still wondering about those fingernails and hearts.
There are so many shades of discolored fingernails.
And just as many discolored hearts.
And I am left to imagine why.
Hmmmm ... Imagine that.

Impressive Isn't It?

If something is difficult to describe
does that make it more enticing to the pen?
To the paper?
To the poet?

If the opening step is miles long
does that make it more intimidating to the runner?
To the climber?
To the nomad?
To the pilgrimage coordinator?

If the sermon is all mythical and difficult to understand
does that make for a more pacified disciple?
An intrigued congregation?
A confused seeker?

I guess it's just a question of how you look at it.
One thing can only exist in relation to another thing
and that puts paid to the concept of separation.

I'm impressed when I hear someone use the word
'flabbergasted' in conversation.
I know what you're thinking ... I'm easily impressed.
Well, yes, I plead guilty. That's true most times.
But that shouldn't take away from the impressive nature
of the use of the word or the person using it.

I would also be impressed if, with a single word,
one could invoke sensory vibrations
and call life itself into being.

Trust me, I've tried, and I've found the only word
with that much power and strength is ... wait for it ...
Poetry. Yes, poetry most definitely and most definitively!
Transcendental, Transitional Meditative poetry!

I'm standing on the corner of Versify and Rhymer,
Prime real estate without doubt,
in the impressive and vibrant neighborhood
of Wild Card Poetry and Kick Ass Prose.
Megaphone in my mind ready to speak,
I'm deep in thought about the true meaning of poetry.

A poem, when the Poetor is creating it,
transports the writer of the word mixtures
to a world apart from this world.
A world of unique singular plurality
decoded from the poet's synaptic mind meanderings,
A world where the poet knows not time or space,
while suspended in that beautiful nether world
of imagination's greatest playground.

A poem, when a Poetee is reading it,
transports the reader of the visual verses
from the mundane to the exhilarating.
A world of painted words sewn to paper
in splashes of eternal synaptic snapshots.
A world where the reader is lost to the world
while interacting with the inner sanctum
and the plurality of the sixth sense.

Poetry!! I am always impressed with that single word.
It reverberates insides of my cranial cage.

Poetry. It invokes sensory vibrations
and calls life itself into being.

Poetry IS the living of words.
The existential living, breathing being of words.

And now ... you're reading THIS poem.
I am impressed!

And my question to you is this.
Are you impressed?

Let's Go, Shall We?

Let's go to the edge and find out why we went there
and why we never went there before.
Shall we?
How do we get there though?
It's a bit of a sticky wicket',
said the croquet ball to the mallet.
And I say to you my tricky little cricket,
'Do we follow lines of longitude and latitude?
Should we hire a rickshaw to take us?
If we just keep walking in circles, headed due west,
would we get there eventually?' Let's start walking.
Shall we?

Well, no matter how we get there,
if we do eventually find the edge
would that prove the earth is flat after all?
Relax, relax, relax.
I'm not saying I'm a flat earth believer.
I just can't shake the desire to find out for myself.
See with my own eyes and the air's ears. Let's go.
Shall we?

Why would I want to do that?
Is that what you're thinking?
    Well here's the deep-dish scoop on that pal.
I've always had this pesky need ... born with it I guess,
bothered with my nose to find things out for myself.
But more often than not when I look for something,
I can't find it. Quite a double bind, huh?
A dead porcupine robbed of all his quills
by some manic-depressive wannabee ink-master
looking for a leg up on a new tattoo.
I hear a new state of the art tattoo salon
opened up in the cross-town Walmart parking lot.
Let's go and get illustrated on the tarmac.
Shall we?

Let's go to a yoga studio and crash a Bikram session.
Shall we?
That could be fun. A real joint jumper,
salt and pepper bone popper and muscle relaxer.
But I should tell you up front,
I'm one of the least flexible people I've ever met.
And I'm prone to passing gas when I stretch.
And I'm prone to passing out in extremely hot rooms.
Having said that, I still think the whole thing would be a gas.
That I can pretty much guarantee in spades.
Yeah. It would be fun for us.
Maybe not for the hot and sweaty folks we'd disturb.
But don't you think people who are way into yoga
tend to take life too seriously?
As a general observation I mean.
I'm sure there are some who would laugh at us
rolling in on them all uninvited and lacking polished social skills.
I'm guessing the instructor would NOT find the humor
in the disruption or our antics. Street people ... us.
I bet we can easily distract him
by making comments about his ponytail and hairline
and that will give us time to escape before they call the fuzz.

We will be blocks away,
sipping on freshly squeezed carrot-ginger juice
and admiring our new tattoos
before they even get there.
This could def be the blockbuster highlight of our day.

Let's go.
Shall we?

Long Before. Long After

Singing in the bathtub on a foggy Wednesday evening
and it feels right. Yeah the feelings tight.
There's a resonance to the sound here.
Too bad there wasn't a tape recorder in here with me right now.
Everything seems to be coming back at me in an echo.
A natural porcelain reverb. A natural high. No lie!
Almost like the opening and closing of an infant's hand.
But really loud like a metal diaper dropping on a tin scale.
And suddenly I start thinking about how mountains
can't be created with words but only by "The Word".
Like poems, short stories, novels and ecstatic love letters.
These are the places we can begin to feel. Rapturously.

But long before they were put into words
mountains were rising from the ocean floors
and piercing the water's surface on their journey skyward.
Long before words.

I'm talking about a time when things were just known.
The times of pure chlorophyll and wild pterodactyl.
The times of wet afternoons in drought riddled dustbowls.
These are all the things that can't be described in words.
They have to be described in vison and touch and smell.
They are ever-changing and with us always
and when you try to tell people this,
some will say you're insane
and some will say congratulations
as if you unlocked some great mystery.

But the mystery is as the mystery does:
A master of sleuth and disguise.
It's impossible for us to track its path or its essence
back to the beginning or on to the end.

It was all there, long before words.
And it will still be there long after words.

Marvelous Fulfillments

It's a marvelous fulfillment,
when I have the occasional original thought.
When it happens,
it feels like someone is slamming a tin hat
right on top of my head
but I wasn't looking and didn't see it coming.
But it's always in a good way.

All sorts of people starve to death or go crazy
in search of original thoughts.
And I'm not claiming to have had many
but I've def had more than my share.
The crazy part is they come more often and with a gusto
when I'm dead broke in pocket, heart and soul.
And I've been dead broke so many times
it kind of feels unnatural when I'm not.

It seems to me that so much of this life
is affected by expectations great and small.
And that makes me think of Dickens.
What the dickens did he know anyway?
Original thoughts! That's what he knew and knew so well.

It's a marvelous fulfillment
when the system tries to test the courage of a weak body
and you weather through it still and take the win.
If there was a soundtrack to such a moment
it might sound like repeating, melancholy piano notes.
Or the sound of a phone ringing too often
after years of not ringing at all.

Either way, that's how I know I'm on my game.
When they test me at my weakest point and I don't fold.

Sometimes a quick glance does the trick.
So if you see me and I'm smiling

but it's the left side of my mouth that's raised...
then you'll know I lost my ace in the hole.
My face will look like the hot steam rising from the coffee truck,
on that morning you REALLY need a java jolt.
To survive.
And get through.

Or it will look like I'm all full up of eggs, T-bone steaks and beer.
And you'll know I didn't fold.

And one last point,
just know I will never beg for mercy.

I've never understood that part of the thing.
And that *'not understanding it'*
is a marvelous fulfillment in and of itself.
.

Not Sorry

Somebody asked me once
to describe the places we do our research.
As writers.
As poets.
As artists.

I told them that it's not really about research.
It's more like being alive and needing to write.
But I meant like *really* needing to write.
As in there isn't another option.
Other than the rope.
The pills.
The bridge.
The gun.

I would apologize for the morose turn we took right there.
If I were sorry.
But you already probably figured out I'm not.
Why does the topic of suicide make people so uncomfortable?
Well, some people that is.
Some look at death as being as natural as living.
And I'm not trying to glorify the act.
I'm just saying that it shouldn't be
the pariah conversation it's made out to be.
But enough about that.

Back to the "life of a writer."
Sounds wonderfully romantic and pretentious, right?
And yes, it's both.
But again, you won't get apologies from me.
Maybe that's what it means to be an artist.
A poet.
A writer.
Not offering so many goddamn apologies to the world.
Just like how I'm not going to apologize for the pint glasses
of limoncello I had for breakfast this morning.

Or the fact that I paired it with a bowl of cottage cheese
and a cucumber and dill and a rooty-toot pill.
Or the fact that I spend most of my time
flipping the pages of books
with words written by women and men long dead now.
Maybe some future generation may flip through pages
and read words written by us after we're long dead and gone.

It's all just a game. A holographic chess game.
It's how you play it that matters in the end.

We are the poets living here and now.
The sons and daughters born of diving inspiration.

We are Monopoly graduates and Risk under-graduates
with a real flair for Scrabble and Sudoku.
We are the card sharks and word magicians.
We are the '*Sorry*' playsters who have the game pegged.
We are the justifiers.
We are the '*Sorry*' masters
and being '*Sorry*' masters means
never having to say sorry.

And we are ... NOT sorry!

Synaptic Synching

They were born on the bright side of a perpetual supernova.
At a very young age, their parents moved them to Evidaris.
The saving grace planet. Their savior. Evidaris.
A world composed of ninety-percent water.
So, all the children were trained very early on
in the revered and sacred art of spirit rowing.
Words and Truka bark canoes were deemed 'Saints'
and were always what they turned to in times of turmoil.
And now, centuries later, two *'Daries'*,
as the locals called themselves, rose above the mists
as primo wordsters and top of the mark rowing stars.
They were known far and wide as 'Sensei and The Professor'
AND
as a word rowing team they were the crème de la crème
rising eloquently above the milky moving mists
excising and exciting the waters they traveled on,
dipping their Truka paddles to just the right depth.
And, with every poem paddle dip
the waters listened intently through shiny dampened ears.
And then just at the exact, precise, correct moment,
the award-winning dynamic paddling duo ,
in the final motions as they crossed the finish line,
would push relentlessly against the grain of the wet
until the waters screamed out in ecstasy
with the lyrics to their national anthem.
Slooshing, pooling and singing in slick harmony.

Professor and sensei you are:
    Too good for words.
    Too broad for describing.
    Too far-out for notions to explain.
    And what will always remain
    inside every ink stain
    is Sensei and The Professor
    forever and ever
    And then longer than that again!

And as the crowd goes wild with delight,
Sensei and the Professor high five each other.
> Sensei whispers to The Professor *'YAY for us'*.
> And The Professor whispers to Sensei

'Let's blow this pop stand Sen.
I can feel a poem comin' on strong
and I want to get it down before it's long gone.'

The crowd looks on in shock and awe
as the dust rises in flashing neon letters and words
of neo-purist profound poetic perfection.
Spreading high and wide and all-consuming
behind the surfboard and land paddles
being wielded in the oh so capable hands
of the Sensei and The Professor disappearing up the hill.

In a roar of serendipitous skull-bending thunder
they ride away on their ink-stained lighting bolt escalator
that leads to the secret vault they keep their far-out words in.
'The S&P Dual Brain of Synaptic Synching'.
   The sign outside reads 'No Trespassing.'

So revered are these two Evidarian bards,
that nobody does trespass.

And so it came to pass that it always was
and will ever be an untouchable place of reverence
housing the sacrosanct words of neo-poetry
proclaiming the SPDBSS is and always will be
the Evidarian Ark of the Covenant.

Happy Corpse

There are no branding irons here.
There are no binding rules here.
Even a sleeping man is still a Buddha, yes?
Makes me call to mind Edgar Cayce, the sleeping prophet.
But don't worry. I wouldn't dare make any predictions in trance.
I only write poems in that state of mind.

Even a sleeping man is still a Buddha, yes?
What is even meant by such a question?
I'm inferring that it means we never really sleep.
Until we do. Right or wrong. Weak or strong.
Now that's something I can dig on my brothers and sisters.
Gravely, ceremoniously in a glad funeral kind of way.
The happy corpse. The happy ghost.
Smiling Buddhas in comatose training.

And as for the living, all the breathing pre-deads:
A poet takes to words.
Like a potter takes to clay.
Like a carpenter takes to wood.
What needs to be done now?
Nothing really.
Just let the words write themselves
into the eternal sleep that isn't sleep.

Two Saturdays ago I swear the breeze smelled just like topaz.
Don't worry. It was a non-metallic wet kind of scent.
I would expect nothing less from the winds
swirling in accordance with historical origins.

So yes, a poet takes to words.
And they take words to places
other than where they usually or often go.
That's the poets' calling.
Even a sleeping poet is still a Buddha. Yes?
A sleeping Buddha that never sleeps!

Relenting Hope

Sensing the shadows in the room growing taller,
I decided to stick my head out the window and look down.
Maybe I was trying to get some air.
Maybe I was hoping to see a woman of distinction in the streets.
Regardless, not finding what I wasn't even looking for,
I sat back down on my bed.
I opened my beer.
I sat there.
And I drank my beer.

Never the victor, never the hero.
But never a loser, never a zero
Today not looking even a little bit like a movie star
More like the pulpy remnants of the OJ bottle bottom.
A quick scan of my room and I see green beer bottles
strewn about but not in any haphazard sort of way.
There was a mad sensibility to how they were laid out.
Something like a miracle. Manna bottles from heaven.
Oh no. They were empty bottles from hell.
In that moment it dawned on me
that I had plenty of bottles and plenty of trouble.

In the room next to me, for hours,
I kept hearing broken glass and screaming.
The couple in that room apparently
had plenty of the same things I had.
I had paid a week's rent three days ago
and I was starting to question
if I would make it the whole week.
I also started to question whether I had parked the car
square in the middle of the street last night.
Blocking all traffic. Blocking festering wilting gardens too.
I vaguely remembered driving home
but couldn't be sure of petty details
like my car's current location.

For some reason I felt so tense in that moment.
The type of tension that often leads to fists pounding on tables.
But sadly, or luckily, my current room
wasn't furnished with any tables.
Just a bed and an uninviting love seat.

So ironic to have a love seat in places like this, I thought.
These were the places where tiresome and angst
was never relenting, but hope sure was.
If it wasn't the part time jobs it was the part time women.
The problem with the women wasn't getting them.
It was getting rid of them when it was time to write.

Psalms to the women I got rid of.
Consoling words to them from me.

Don't cry ladies. You're better off without me.
You'd always have to doubt me
and the odd things all about me.
Count up your blessings tonight
while I sit alone but not lonely and write.
Say good riddance to that poem writing dope
who lived his life in relenting hope.
He was never right in the wrong of the thing
And never wrong when he'd solemnly sing:
Goodnight, Lady. It's time to say goodnight
It's half-past time for this joy boy to write
of a life truly misspent in relenting hope
and a minion who never got to meet the Pope.

Amen.

Revelations Round About Midnight

In my experience I've found that no amount of persuasion
can convince a fool of his folly.
I've been on both the trying to convince
and trying to be convinced end of said scenario.
So I'm confident in the credibility
of the opening line statement of this poem.
I'm also confident that the forest is livelier
the moment you suddenly realize
that there was never anything to realize.
And that's saying a lot. Isn't it?

At midnight, about two or three nights ago,
I was passing through a lovely little garden.
Underneath the lamplight lantern glow,
The professor was there. And Sensei was there too.
When I saw them, I asked what they were up to.
The Professor said, "we're discussing a double bind koan.
Then Sensei said "we've been here for hours
and haven't yet found a solution."
I put on my best Geoffrey Rush voice and said,
'Yes, mmh-hmm, it's a bit of mystery I say,
mmh-hmm, mmh-hmm a bit of a mystery, isn't it?'
Then in a harmonic unison they both blurted out,
"Yes, it is! Isn't it wonderful?"

I asked them if they had ever tried some foliage reading?
In response Sensei said, "The yellow leaves never do the trick."
"How'd you know I was thinking yellow leaves?" I asked
Sensei smiled a wicked little glad-ass grin and said,
"If you were an Evi - darian, it would be Evi – dent.
I'm Evidarian and so it was blatantly evident to me."
I said, in my best John Wayne A-mur-kan drawl,
"Well, liddle lady, I'm from Missouri ... show me.
She then proceeded to screech three times,
blow on a yellow leaf and ignite it to red, then it burnt out,
and then the ashes restructured and turned emerald-green.

At that point I was definitely a believer.
That Evidarian blow blew all the cobwebs from my mind;
actually blew them right out of my visible universe.

Now here's the poop ... the real scoop:

I've seen many midnights come and go.
I've seen The Professor take over the show.
I've seen Sensei play Stradivarius violins
dressed up in indigenous buffalo skins.
But I've never bore witness to such a queer sight
as Sensei and The Professor round about midnight
trying to provoke a new kind of light
into an original paradoxical riddle
to calculate the square root of Sensei's fiddle.
But alas there was no logical reasoning.
No winter to pepper summer with seasoning.

On that hazy midnight a revelation was revealed
and to this very day my lips remain sealed.

The Professor and Sensei spilled the secrets of death
and pinpointed the original birth of our breath.

Big deal some might say; and they might be right,
but those are the rounders who never see the light
or that shining revelation round about midnight
when Sensei and The Professor flash into sight.

Ruminating on Nothing

I've heard of entire lifetimes spent ruminating on deficiencies.
These are the things I cry for.
Imagine being at peace with nothing your whole life?
Look, I'm not saying I'm some sort of
Paramahansa Yogananda or anything like that.
I'm just saying I'm glad I'm able to let things go sometimes.
I don't want to be like that mosquito that spent its life
trying to feed off the iron bull. Getting a skunk pull.
I don't want to be like the seeker who was tone deaf
to the booming of a distant bell.

I heard a story once of this bullfrog who went to Kyoto
to study universal and timeless truths.
And I guess it was a big deal because
from the standpoint of the bullfrog community
it meant a lot to finally have one of their own
be able to hear the sound of one hand clapping.

There does come a critical point in any poem
where the reader should be asking themselves ... *"wait, what?"*
Maybe a poet owes that to their literary recipient.
Mebbee ... Mebbee not.
I'm just making observations
from my heart and mind over here.
You'll have to give me at least a little bit
of room for my Zen antics.

Anyway, the point of the story is that this bullfrog
is said to have found an old Chinese Master
hiding up the sleeve of his kimono.
Then this one day when he found himself
in the presence of a Sabre-Toothed Tiger with a toothache
a mother of a toothache, and in a hell of a mood to boot,
Perfect timing? Well ...
sh into sight... sh into shrines ... sh into Shinto
Shingo, Wingo, Dingo, Flamingo

Buck naked bullfrogs and slant eared gollywogs
hiding under stone faced water-logged crab carcasses.
He pulled on the loose string of the kimono
and out jumped the Chinese Kung-Fu Master.
Some thought him a real Fuk-Yu Master.
And that he was. The tiger didn't know what he was in for.

The Sabre-Toothed Tiger snarled and snapped.
The Fuk-Yu Master screamed and yapped.
and somehow in the middle of this bizarre cacophony
they found a genetic, phonetic understanding,
way down yonder on the quantum level near old New Jersey
where quarks and muons dance the boot scootin' boogie
and rock the jungle to the vine with melancholy roars.
If you don't know how to get there and need directions
Just ask Freddie 'boom' Cannon where it's at.
He's a seasoned Palisade 'Park-er'. An unlicensed car-jockey.
He knows where everything's at. He knows everything
but he really knows nothing the best. That's his forte.
Maybe he's a Fuk-Yu shapeshifting master in disguise.

The Fuk-Yu Master and the Sabre-Toothed Tiger
became the best of jungle jivin' buddies
and loosey-goosey vine-swingin' Tarzan wannabes
for a short while and then they regained their sanity
and parted ways and wished each other well.
The Master went back to the kimono sleeve
and the Tiger went back to the jungle.

Today they are still pen pals writing once a month.
They sometimes celebrate Christmas and Easter
with their, outside the inner circle, friends and miscreants.
But no matter what the occasion or non-occasion
they both agree the best times they ever spend are the times
they spend together ruminating on nothing
and noting each rumination's depth of nothingness
hoping to one day find a new kind of black hole
that holds the key to an even deeper kind of nothing
that holds the everything and the all.

Scheme of Things

Just as I would surely recognize a rainbow in the eye of a hurricane.
I would also surely recognize you if I saw you in pure spirit form.
It would be a beautiful sight if I were to bear witness
as the skin separates and you flow right into the spirit.
Would it be any different if it happened standing in the moonlight?
By the seaside? In an airport? On a racetrack?
Would it be any different if no one else was around
to hear the waves crash? The sky fall? The mountains crumble?
Would any of this even matter at all
in the scheme of things.

Some creative types don't realize they're creative
until they're older and more life-seasoned.
Less intimidated and less sense reasoned.
Maturity being the essence of the matter here.
That's just how these things happen sometimes.
in the scheme of things.

Lately I've been hanging my brain on a trick hat rack
like a crazy mixed up ring-a-ding-ding king
betting on roulette sitting at the craps table.
The words fluke and chance kept dancing in tandem
with each throw and bounce-back of the dice.
Building a jigsaw crossword right behind my eyeballs.
I mean I could see all the words inside my head.
I wanted to reach my fingers into my eye sockets
to grab the words but decided it was enough
just to know they were there if and when I needed them
like a get out of jail free card in a monopoly prison town.
It would give me leverage to chisel my way out of trouble
in the scheme of things.

Straight lines, curves, black and whites and colors
Dr. Suess, Disney, Roadrunner and Bugs.
They're all right there for the watching
in cinemascope tunnel vision dreams

and that makes everything air-tight, outta sight.
Alright, alright, alright light the pipe
smoke the bite and *'thole the kitly'**
to keep it tight in the scheme of things.

The scheme is usually written in stone and unalterable.
It's the left hand of destiny that can't turn right.
It's the right hand of karma that won't turn left.
It's the broken steering wheel of the gods gone crazy
guiding a Cheshire cat to sad morose movies
and banning him from the best comedy clubs in town.
It's the perversity personified that always remains anonymous
in the scheme of things.

And, in the scheme of things,
there is no real scheme.
It's just a bunch of things rattling around
in this dented and bent hubcap we call life.
We keep spinning and grinning and spinning
like an old worn-out porcupine that's lost all its quills
moving at breakneck speed going nowhere fast.

We're the doped-up needle in the compass
that always points to magnetic north
trapped in this eternal loop.
An unanswerable riddle
stuck in the middle.
A twist and a shout
with no way out,
in the scheme of things.

'thole the kitly' is Scottish Gaelic for 'stand the tickling.'

Some Ancient Fellow

Exaggerated forms of the thinnest of lines
are appearing everywhere to me these days.
I've spent eons trying to clean up my problem life.
But that's where I have to pose the question.
What is the problem singular, and what are the problems plural.
You can't repair a faulty circuit in the dark.
And you can't play hockey in a field of wild horses.
And I can't fix my problem if I don't know what my problem is,
or even if I have one.

The sages say you can't command a genuine response
if you don't ask a genuine question.
And you can't force a passionate kiss.
It has to be completely spontaneous to be real.

I say you can't build a birdhouse inside a tire.
And you can't ride a bicycle with broken wheels.
And you can't make a T-Bone out of hamburger.
And you can't make me believe I have a problem.

Sometimes I do resort to desperate and dangerous methods.
hoping for fixed answers to flexible questions.
Here are some atypical examples:
Commander Whitehead has a beard.
Why does he have no face?
Fred Astaire was a great dancer.
Why did he have no legs?
The United States President was born in 2099.
Why is he dead when the world is alive?

And it just goes on and on and on
like a never-ending nonsensical rubber soul song.
The questions present themselves all in the plural.
The flexible answers are caged in the singular.
And I think it was all invented by the moronic sidekick
of some ancient fellow with dementia.

Some Footprints

I heard the best radio interview recently. It was on NPR.
Terry Gross was the interviewer.
Danny Trejo was being interviewed.
It so fascinated me, his story.
From prison to the bright lights of Hollywood.
What a change in ranks and levels!

I heard the greatest compliment recently.
Someone said to a gas station cashier they see on a regular basis,
"You rarely seem to lose the meditations ever, if at all."
In that moment I remember thinking that the people
who hold out for better don't always get it.
And those who jump at the first option don't always get it right.
Maybe all things come back again. Mebbee they don't.
But I tell you, with confidence, some footprints were meant to last.

I ate the most savory and memorable soufflé just yesterday.
I can't remember for the life of me what was in it.
So I was compelled to go back today and order another.
When I got there, as if they were trying to be more mysterious,
I was told they only make their souffles one time only.
Then I did what we all do.
Tried to make sense of the nonsense,

So I went back again the next day prepared for history.
I took my shoes with fresh blood-soaked soles
out of my garbage lined backpack.
Put them on and walked around the place nonchalantly,
knowing that someday in the far distant future
there would be a murder committed there
the police would attend,
and the floor would be sprayed with luminal,
and MY footprints would come to life again
in shining neon blue living-color.
Some footprints are meant to last.
Mine will be one of them.

Something Like

Something like eyes out of focus.
Or a new dance move you haven't caught up with yet.
Everything exists in a certain way. Ok, here's the idea.
You can meditate if you want to, that's fine.
Me? I just never could. Lord, I tried. Believe me, I've tried.
I did hear once, while waiting at the train station,
that "no brick has ever been polished to make a mirror."
The moment I heard it I knew I was hearing something poetic.

Something like visiting a local strawberry farm in the winter months.
Right when you were starting to eat less and less red meat.
Only to find that they have no strawberries for sale.
In fact, they look at you like you're crazy to think they would in fact
have strawberries for you to buy in January.
Then the billiard balls start banging around upstairs in your brain and
you realize you aren't in Florida anymore.
Of course you can't get strawberries in January in Kalamazoo.
What were you thinking?

Yeah, something like that.
Just not in the ordinary sense of the word.
Have you ever had a moment when you found it a bit difficult to say
what you're thinking? You're not alone.
Believe me, you're in good company actually.
We've all had interdimensional déjà vu moments.
Something like being Jughead when Archie says "Whuzzup?"
Something like swimming in an air-filled concrete pool.
Something like flying too close to the ground
when a gopher pokes his head up and knocks you senseless.

Yeah, we've all experienced something like that.
And *a man's a man for a' that and a' that*.
Rest in peace Robbie. Your candle still Burns.
Your poems were meant to last, and they did.
Your footprint was meant to last, and it did.
Something like eternal life in perpetual resurrection.

Sometimes It Happens

A layman says much from the shallows after deep sessions
of trigonometric electric conversations from inner space.
"Thoughts aren't entities, so why bother about such things?"
I suppose we need not bother. I'm ok with that.
Pause. But then again I'm not ok with that.

All you see and hear doesn't need to be well understood.
WYSIWYG = What you see is what you get.
and you can usually touch and talk to what you see.
until it's dead and gone. And then you don't see it anymore.
But while it is here in our scope of vision, it is an entity.
And who's to say it's not an entity if we can't see it.
It could still be vibrating on a different string of existence.
If we can see it we can describe it, so it is real to us.

What you hear is intangible but is something understood.
You can't see it or touch it but you can converse with it.
Same thing for the thoughts. You can hear your own thoughts
and sometimes can sense other's thoughts ... just know them.
Extra Sensory Perception is being in touch with thoughts
traveling on the vibration of strings, and sometimes tied together.
So thoughts have indivisible, invisible bulk and weight.
They are unseen entities, but entities just the same.
We need to come to terms with the unseen and non-vocal.
And when we can do this and be at ease with the revelation
we will be more fully human and more fully spirit.
In this way we will remain undisturbed.
At home in and out of our skin whether awake or asleep.
We will have created your own Nirvana
where we can be alone with our sight and mind.
Or we can invite other sighters and minders in
for a drink of thought conversations or simple sight-seeing.
We can also join vibratory groups like bird watching and hearing.

Alright then, do you remember sitting tranquilly meditating
with an incense stick burning sweetly in front of you.

in the presence of the old masters and gurus
seeing and listening to what wasn't there,
but you knew it was really there in its invisible form.
Maybe that's the point of meditation,
the self-medicated sedation of expectation.

I'm going to digress for a moment to paint a word picture
of what I mean so you can really *'get it'*.

I knew this beer loving gal with two new hips.
She was kind of a fierce thing in a gentle sort of way.
She walked a bit funny but otherwise was easy on the eyes.
We were connected on a string we couldn't see or hear.
But somehow we did see and hear each other's thoughts.
I would think something, and she would think it at the same time
or receive it in double quick no time at all delivery.
in exactly the same déjà vu all-knowing sense.

Has that ever happened to you?
Not the getting new hips and loving beer thing.
But the thought exactness.
The thought exchange immediacy is what I mean.
That goosebumps, hair-raising all-knowing feeling
When you are actually a part of it.
That's what I'm talkin' about ...

Sometimes it happens.

Only an Ism Away

If you don't mind, I'd like to talk a bit about ifanisms.
So I'll start. What really is this universe after all?
Is it a mechanism, a checkanism, a what the heckanism
or just a tainted jury rigged gamanism??
If it's not that, what is it? Who knows? Who cares!

I do have deep respect for things at odds with themself.
Like a monarchistic republic or a republican socialist.
Like lava flow or a crumbling mountain.
Like a fabulous off-key singer or a keyed-up virtuoso.
Like a fiery black hole or a dark charcoal sun.
I'm sinking, sinking, sinking ... sinking deeper
into a divine juxtaposed contradiction.

For the purposes of separating sanity from insanity
you could argue that black is white and red is green
and there's nary another color in between.
There isn't a black-white but there IS a red-green.
That's right! That culpable northern TV miscreant.
Red Green and nephew Harold and all their shenanigans
come directly to you from the inner sanctum of the Possum Lodge.
Like, it could totally be considered mythical,
but in an even more powerful sense it's almost backwoods mystical.
This is just another one of those "crazy ideas of the world"
that somehow came to fruition and kind of infected us
so we'd be addicted with their needle of nonsense
and be forced to tune in to watch them every week.
But I must admit there are things I like about the show.
Like the way Red always signs off to end every show.
'Remember men ... If women don't find you handsome
they should at least find you handy.'
And Harold. Dear insipid ridiculous Harold
with his ghetto blaster strapped on like an axe.
He just rolls his eyes and finger-flicks a button for loud music
when he doesn't like what '*Unc*' is spewing.
And then he chuckles that goofy pukey-type guffawing laugh

and his eyes bug out and his overbite ambushes his grin
and his whole body just shakes like he's havin' a sneizure
when the nose-busting *'achoos'* gang up on each other.
I tell ya, if he ain't the goofiest looking idiot you ever saw
... well then.... I guess I never wrote a poem.

Sorry ... my train jumped the rails there for a bit,
but getting back on the ifanisms track,.
I'm wondering ... is it me or does hope
sometimes come shaped almost like a fan?
Like the "fan" in the word "i-fan-isms"
You can get rid of the i-isms and keep the fan.
Sort of separate the men from the boys.
Why? I'll tell you why.
Because hope does sometimes come shaped like a fan.
Because a fan can cool a hot head.
And a fan can give hope to a rising star
starting out at the bottom rung on the ladder.

Because all coinisms have two distinct sides.
and both sides have been minted with hope embedded,
And *'ifan'* you ever need a hand up from the deep water
remember hope floats.
And ... the hope fan is only an *'ism'* away.

The Cold Nights of Albuquerque

I've lain down in beds bred by the cold nights of Albuquerque.
In hobo towns and hotel dives that were anything but turn-key.
I've spent some long hot nights bummin' in Miami.
Put down roots for a week. Had nowhere else to be.
Layin' stretched out jacuzzi style on the sizzlin' beach,
oglin' the lookers, floozy style. Those I think I can reach.

And I've spent temperate nights in southern Oregon
leavin' my mark stamped on hearts before I moved along.
And then there were those boozy nights I didn't have a clue
walkin' on the stocking pokin' through the shoe.
Wishin' on a star ... third one in the little dipper.
Feelin' like a sorry horse who lost his metal slipper.

Some nights turn tough and sometimes life gets rough
and I never know where I'll lay me down
Now a couple of skipped meals and a hundred freight trains later
I got booted off the freighter in good old Albuquerque.
Good thing I'd grabbed an extra pack of extra hot beef jerky.
I'll have to dust the dusty roads with my broken shoes
heading to the campsite where I've already paid my dues.
I'll scoff a pair of long johns somewhere along the way.
I've been here before and it ain't no place to go.
I've spent too many hard cold nights here in New Mexico
runnin' from a posse of relentless wind and snow.
Yeah ... believe me. it does snow here from time to time
and when it does you can bet it's always unexpected.
But I'm a savvy savant so I expect the unexpected.
Hence the booze and long johns in my trusty, dusty backpack
and my ornamental key ring with the mini-mike car jack.

I find a spot for my bedroll in the heart of hobo hollow
near a humming fellow squatter. A real hard act to follow.
So I introduce myself and ask him for his name.
I offer him a handshake and a friendly swig of whiskey.
He looks at me through glassy eyes, softly slurs "which key?"

I'm guessing he's either slightly deaf or really stinkin' drunk.
It seems like either one or both would be a sure-fire bet.
He chooses not to grab onto the offered olive branch.
So I tie my skivvies on the crowbar layin' by his side,
and wave it high above my head in a fake surrender.

If you think it's a symbol of defeat, brother you'd be wrong.
I'd just be me working out an imaginary new drum sequence
for my adaptation of The Battle of New Orleans.
And then lookie here, comin' round the bend is none other than
Johnny Horton in a grisly white-ass patched up suit.
He's got Johnny Reb two-step skippin' by his side
and by God they've got a honky tonkin' big ass croc in tow
with a cannonball stuck up his rectum... which brings me to recall
an old ass joke I used to know but can't remember how it starts.
I recall the punchline is *"rectum ... nearly killed 'im."*

Okay enough of all this noopid, toopid nonsense.
I'm cold and I'm tired and I'm hungry and thirsty,
but even worse than that, I just can't believe I'm here.
Doing what I swore I'd never do again ...
spending me another hard day's night
in the cold nights of Albuquerque.

The Gods Are Not Crazy

I want to be cool about it.
I want to stay in the moment for a bit.
Grab a baseball bat for a home run hit.
But I find it non-astonishing and underling admonishing
that the bosses of the world are in it for themselves?

Me? I'm astonished when an ivory tower dweller
even recognizes the face or knows the name of an underling.
And in the midst of these thoughts, my 5 years old daughter
shows me a big lopsided grin and her first wiggly tooth
with the hopes of garnering a visit from the tooth fairy.

And in that moment I realize I don't ever want to be a boss.
I love knowing and greeting people by name.
And I love being shown wiggly teeth from my kids.
And I realize the meaning of life.

It's not a coke bottle thrown from a helicopter.
And it's not an uneducated African tribesman
who talks in a quaint tongue-clicking language,
picking the bottle up and travelling for miles trying to return it
to the God's in the helicopter who lost it.

I realize the Tooth Fairy is a kind angelic spirit.
AND the Gods are not crazy.

The Unison of Opposites
(aka Im Com Re Ex)

The same ends of a magnet (north/north) push apart
but a quick draw McGraw flick of the wrist and the opposite ends
(north/south) crash together in a silent metal ecstasy.
What a balancing act.
Like when two people have nothing in common,
but can't help but find each other undeniably attractive.
It's like when two differing notions
somehow imply each other without meaning to.
A real encounter of forces, right?
Coming from opposed realms but providing completion
instead of repulsion.
These are the fundamental first games of energies destined.
Impel. Compel. Repel, Expel.

Now, let's separate the first syllables from the "pels".
We have *Im, Com Re Ex.* Could be the vocal key to many things.
Memorize it this way: (*I'm Composing Red Expletives*)
So if a criminal mind type holds a gun to your head
and says "get ready to kiss your ass goodbye loser"
all you have to scream is *"Im Com Re Ex,"*
and he'll eat the gun and blow his dickhead to oblivion.

Remember these syllables: *In Com Re Ex*.
They could very well save your life in a pinch.

And no matter how you mix them up,
nobody can't make sense of them. But YOU can.
The words are all powerful sans their first syllable.
They need the 'pel' to give them direction, instruction.
But when you leave it off you become the director
and they must obey your every silent mind command.

Really, everything in our realm is down to
the upside heavy duty over-bosses: North and South!
East or West just don't have the chutzpah to attract or repel.
They are the nothing nobodys of the magnetic world.

They just got no magnetism at all...
never did have ... never will have.

So now let's get back to basics and what really counts.
Let's go back to the Poles. The Polar opposites.

Those that get really stuck on each other
are the over magnetized Magma-maniacs of the world.
Some folks are very scared of these powerful people
who distill their own aphrodisiacs in their synapses.
Everyone finds them unavoidably attractive
and in truth the attraction usually overcomes folks' fears
and they take a chance, have the dance hoping for romance.

We were taught to be in awe of attraction.
and most of the time the intention behind it doesn't matter.
But when the baby starts laughing all of a sudden it matters.
And you are so happy when you hear that laughter you cry.
Thinking, thank God the baby didn't get thrown out
accidentally with the bath water. You sigh with relief.

At this point in their young tadmadish lives they are so removed
from really knowing what it's all about and seeing this innocence
shining in their big as saucers eyes agog with wonder,
you can't help but recall how it feels
to be tadmadish for a moment too.

That's the unison of opposites I was talkin' about.
I knew a guy once who used to say that.
And he used to say, very adamantly too,
that misspellings are in their own way correct.
Probably more correct than the commonly accepted spellings.

I, for one, believe he is right.
And Mebbee he is.
Mebbee ... Mebbee not.

Thick in the Middle

The clouds and the mountains.
The trees and the people.
Only one of the aforementioned tries to still the process.
and control the process. I'll let you guess which one.

Now then, have you ever tried to take control
of something that wiggles?
Like trying to pick up a flopping fish?
That's how this poetry thing feels sometimes.
And other times it's as easy
as counting the number of holes in a net.
It's the fine art of measuring the world with words.

I think I woke up way out on the fringe this morning.
Like a bottle of ink thrown at a wall.
Thick in the middle then spread out after that.
The outer part is where the more complicated patterns emerge.
The thick middle part is more like a person
who's hostile toward nature.
Why on earth would someone want to beat nature up?
Be hostile toward nature?   Beats me.

It's so funny when people say,
"we are so smart we're even able to travel in space."
Aren't some of us in space already?
Here on earth where it's thick in the middle
of the scratch and scarce.

I don't know about you, but I'm in a space all my own,
in the middle of the thick and happy as a pig in shit.

So, please don't come knockin'
'cause there ain't nobody home but us poets
and we prefer our own company most times,
Especially when we're deep down, high-wire clown,
hole in the net in the middle of the thick.

Title
(no, seriously, that's the title)

It always starts with a title.
Sometimes it's just a placeholder word or phrase.
Sometimes I sit totally blank, so I just type "title"
at the top of a page on a computer screen.
Sometimes It's the only way I can get the thing going.
I've tried other ways and methods. No joy.

It's so bizarre. Like a Marezy Doats and Dozey Doats
kind of mixed-up surreal moment that equals nada.
The engine won't rev until there's that pesky placeholder
sitting up there, all high and mighty, at the top of the page.

So just know and understand that's how this one started.
That's enough misdirected attention for right now.
Any more of this bluster and I'm risking leaving no time
for the building up of the thing I want to build..
This is making me think of Steve Richmond
and his Gagaku poetry.

He attempted to live by a rule of methods and no methods.
Simultaneously. That's my take on it at least.

When I first heard of Gagaku poetry
I thought it might be Haiku poetry to puke by.
Zen avter vat zeemed like zenturies in meditation
I realized somebody should start a new kind
of short, slap my face twice to wake me up, poetry.
And then I thought... well... why not me?

I think I'd call it poo-etry or Haipu-ke.
The only saving grace Haiku has, is that it has no titles.
I have too much to say to try to say it in 17 syllables.
Hell, 700 syllables many times isn't enough for me
to be able to say what I want to say in a poem.
Life is a complex arrangement of simplicities.

A paradox for the mind frame to cozy up to.

Maybe it's too fundamental to give titles after all.
A certain pre-ordained amount is sufficient to manage.
But the excess is what burdens a man.

I wonder if Hank would care about any of this.
That's a question we'll never know the answer to.
He's a Long-Gone Lonesome Daddy now.

It waxes blurred poetics that so much we long to know,
will never be able to be known.

There's only one thing we can know for certain,
an old Hank nailed it real good when he sang,.
"I'll Never Get Out of This World Alive."

So now I take off my poet's hat
and put on my Pastor's collar and robe.
I hold my latest poetry book high and say,
'Amen to that brothers'n'sisters ...
just plain and simple AMEN to that!'

'Bless you all and thanks for lisn'n
Y'all come back soon now ...Ya hear?'

Truth or Consequences

Have you ever seen two sticks standing up against each other?
This one I know is truth.
I've seen the consequences of such a thing.
If you take one away, the other one falls.
Any good stick stander would know this.
But it's not too different from what happens inside the skin.
It's all happening under there.
In there. A real miraculous type of thing.

It's like when the Pacific Ocean blows you a misty kiss
and it feels like it was meant and sent
just to you to soothe your fevered brow; cool you right down
and all the skin on your face starts crying joy beads of tears.
Or when you feel like a restless pair of legs
dangling over the edge of something into empty space
where they are free from fear and can never cramp.

Seriously. It feels like the natural flow of water
and then it goes on for some time after that.
I'm sure I could feel it today and totally forget it
and yet still recognize it tomorrow.
But I also know that no water ever stays put. It can't.
Well, some can. Those backwater town olden day pools
Turned killer by bacteria infested choleric stagnant water.
Whenever I think about that I always find it sickening.
Excuse the pun. It was just me trying to be punny-funny.
I know you're shaking your head in disgust at that attempt.
Oh well just another failure in a long line of failures for me.

But enough about water and don't get me started on Kotter.
Left school long ago. The seats, blackboards and detentions.
So now onto a very interesting, mind-boggling subject.
Poets. They come in many garden varieties and styles,
and no poet's mind ever stays still ... ever! I know.
I'm one of those renegade ball-busting podium lovers.
And I know how to bump and grind the pages to dance.

There's just way too many words and letters and numbers
swirling around in the ether just waiting to be caught,
whispering sweet nothings in my ears .. *'Pick me. Pick me.'*
Then louder, *'For God's sake have mercy. Pick me.'*

So I pick up my pen and put down my thoughts
on a smudgy napkin or piece of wrinkled toilet paper,
depending on where I am when the words call to me.
They can be such unwelcome voyeurs at times
and other times they are like a long-lost friend come home.

The truth is, you have to be ever vigilant and always listening
so you will hear the words when they come calling.
If you are lackadaisical and mind chasing rainbows
The consequence is ... no poetry today baby.

Kids used to play a game back in the 50s called.
"Heavy, heavy hangs over thy head"
There main revolving players were a guesser and an asker
and the extras were kids waiting for their turn.
The guesser was blindfolded and sitting on a chair
with the asker standing behind the guesser
dangling an object over the guesser's head.
The guesser could ask 10 questions
and after that had to guess what it was.
To this day I'm sure a kid who played this game,
way back when, was the driving force behind the TV show
Truth or Consequences.

I realize this is definitely a questionable accusation I've made.
Suggesting the birth of this program was a blatant result of
out and out dad-nab-it vile and vicious plagiarism
and an absolute dead to rights case for child abuse
(stealing game precepts from innocent children)
I might be accused of consorting with my foreign contacts,
to ask them to partake in the most diabolical meddlings,
singling out my contacts "the Russians", or "the Chinese".
The former being dyed-in-the-wool, die-hard Stalinists.
And the latter, even worse, the Wuhan wet-market mongers.

and if I was a senator or congressman, there would likely be
a congressional investigation into my poems, my poetry
my music, and my whole life from soup to nuts. No pun intended.

In the end, it all comes down to Truth or Consequences,
and I'll take consequences every time.
Life's too short to be the dull side of the knife.

Danger is my unwritten middle name
and I want to live on the sharp side of the blade.
I want to REALLY live before I say my final Sayonara.

So slice away baby ... just slice away.
I'm always more alive when I bleed.

Vague and Prickly

Particles or waves?
Which is the idealist looking for?
Some like it vague.
But the prickly people are a precise people.
You've got to be prickly sometimes.
And you've got to be wide and wondering sometimes too.
Those are basically the two kinds.
Both are valuable in my eyes.

Doesn't it feel like it's been an incredibly long time
since we've paid enough proper attention
to old ladies and wishful thinkers?
Sounds like another one of my hardheaded theories, right?
I swear it's not.

By the way, who started it? Everything I mean.
And was the Myth of Sisyphus really a myth or eerily true?
Camus knew there was only one real question.
I haven't decided my answer just yet.
Just remember, not answering it won't get rid of it.
And also, by the way ... who was the first person
to make it so acceptable as to use BTW.
Was it Some texter called Dexter sitting next store to Camus?
Anyhow, we all know it means 'by the way' BUT
it could be so very many things pleasant and unpleasant:
Broken tires wobble. bring the whistle.
Bark twice wonce. Be the woke.
Black tives watter. Bonkers this week.
And I could go on forever and ever and even longer.
But, I don't want to bore you, so I won't.

Last night I swear I heard some screaming in the streets.
It sounded like someone was saying,
"the sea would never be worried
that the wave would someday disappear."
(I wondered for a moment if it was Buddha's ghost.)

The screaming Mimi in the streets just went on and on and on.
It was as if someone took out a full-page yell with the town crier.
Then they started screaming something about "the original bang."
I couldn't quite make it all out, but it seemed like the gist was,
we are all structures in space. And we are all portions of time.
But we still don't even know how to define ourselves.
Structurally (form) or proportionately (form in respect to space).
I look at it like a pie (structure). Me, one of 12 pieces (portion).

But structure and portion aside,
we still don't know what happened
before the first thing ever happened.
The bang that everyone calls the 'big' bang.
And how do we know it was a BIG bang?
In the grand scheme of things, it could be a small bang
in a super-humongous conglomeration of multiverses.
You know what I mean?

Like, that original force.
Or particle. Or wave. Or a particle-wave.
Or whatever Carl Sagan saw and said
when Mutt Sever eyed the telescope thread
and deduced gravity is a push not a pull.
Makes sense to me like magnetic polar sames.
They push away and keep their distance.
But with a pull they collide into each other.
They're iron, so they don't explode.
Planets and solar systems would explode and disintegrate
if indeed gravity is a pull force.
And if it is a push force as I purport, a horse of a different color,
then the solar system, galaxies and universes remain stable-ish
and we live and breathe and go on as before ad perpetuum.

In a vague and prickly way ... that is.

When the Wind Drops

The wind drops.
Sometimes at the perfect time.
Sometimes when it's least expected.
But it drops because that's its nature.

I remember this one day in September
when the leaves kept on falling
and the flowers kept on calling
and somewhere down in Texas
I just knew the dogies were bawling.
All because the wind was dropping.
And this piqued my interest because the mountains
become more mysterious during the times of wind drop.
On these days, more often than not,
you may find a sparrow twittering somewhere behind you.
The best part is, this happens because the wind rules
and requires no intention on your part to drop.

From a deconstructionist perspective,
it's what happens between the sounds
that you're going to want to hear very distinctly
and pay closest attention to.
Higher levels are developed from that kind of insight.
They take their flavor from that sort of thing.

Let's jump forward to a moment ago once again.
The wind continued its dropping performance.
And I was nursing a great gimlet in a glass goblet.
It was my third drink, so I was in no hurry.
Gin can have that effect on a person.

Looking deeply into my drink
and savoring the flavor of the wind
I started thinking about Cotton Ginny and wondering.
Was she a Gin drinker? A gimlet girl?
Or just a simple cotton gin operator of old,

spending her days separating cotton fibers from seeds.
Or was she an oceanographer, separating divers from weeds
in the watery depths of her Caribbean cranium?
Or was she just a plain old cotton picker named Ginny.

I like to think she was an inventor of original dreams.
A tee shirt kind of gal sowing fashion to the masses.
And then graduating to teaching cotton-picking classes
that required all the students to wear stereo glasses
The wrap around molly-goggle type of protective shades
so they wouldn't be blinded by the light of her vibrant intellect
and they'd be able to easily cotton-on to the course being taught.

I just felt a weakening of the breeze on my neck
and I have an inkling the wind is going to drop,
so, I bare my mast, curl the cloth and batten down the hatches.
Don't want anything to take the wind out my sails.
But I guess that's impossible. Wind can't be caught or contained
and Donovan did have it right after all,
when he so esoterically sang ...
'Ah but I may as well try and catch the wind'.
Which, BTW, actually is grammatically incorrect.

To be grammatically correct, it should be,
'Ah but I may as well try *'to'* catch the wind,'
But to be musically correct in a flowing way, it should be,
'Ah but I may as well try *'and'* catch the wind.'

But that's really neither here nor there. Is it?
The only thing that's important today is,
when the wind drops. And you might ask 'Why?'

Well, when the wind drops the music starts
and my drink gets topped up
and all's right with the world ...
when the wind drops.

Ahhh yes ... when the wind drops.

What's Left

What's left of what was originally there?

It's not advisable to spill the pint glass of wine
on the keyboard or the iPhone.
But it is advisable to cease and desist from something,
if you've hated every minute of it.
And it might be wise to live life along your own lines.
Some folks flourish well beyond their work.
and others get stuck in the sticky muck of the back-end kick up.

What's left of the adulation missed by the former child star?
It's obnoxious to fall victim to fame and inflate the ego,
but they do at the time and then miss it at some later time.
I wonder ... would I react any different? Would you?

Nothing seems to last anymore. Not even tattoos are permanent.
Did you know lasers are available
that will remove some well imbedded ink?
These are the things that make me want to check out early.
And sometimes early is right on time.

But I can't checkout early because, because, because ...
I just started getting calls to do poetry readings.
They said they can't pay me an appearance fee
but they can offer me free drinks all night. Yayah!!
They sure got me pegged. That's right up my alley.
To me that's a currency I appreciate and understand.
So before checking out I have to take advantage of the free drinks
and the continental breakfast that will offer eggs benedict
and an omelet station as it's highlights. I'm diggin' it already.

You wouldn't miss that either would you.
Don't lie.
I mean, after free drinks
and the ultimate in continental breakfasts ...
What's left?

What Then?

There are definite shapes and forms,
like whirlpools in water, of eddies in streams,
or a beatnik on the edge of a riverbank.
Who would have thought a beatnik
would be wasting the day away on a riverbank.

Not I, not the whirlpools or the water.
And the sun keeps waxing hotter and hotter..

On this day I've gathered all the cosmic rays in sight,
hoping to find the vantage points and underlying hints
of common-sense scenarios from other galaxies.
Whether intellectual or psychological or spiritual or physical.
And what, if anything, does that mean.
Would it be disappointing if I said it means nothing?.
And everything? All at once, yet separate in its unity?
I'm getting a headache and a throat-crave.
So let's not talk about this anymore right now.
Otherwise we'll go out of our heads and die of thirst.

Back to a different point. Isn't it like a dream?
Really though. It's like a dream sometimes.
Where we're all taking our sweet time to take on our forms.
Each one of us. And yet from another vantage point, none of us.
Well now, where should we go from here? Somewhere? Or nowhere.

And the whirlpool keeps dancing around in the water.
And the sun keeps waxing hotter and hotter.

And what if it turns out I'm that beatnik on the riverbank?
Out of place and out of time. Here, but really there.
What if I end up walking stride for stride with the Tigris Euphrates?
What if I dissolve into its viscosity and become a whirlpool?

What then? I ask you.
What then???

DOUBLE TROUBLE

Author Profile

Jose & James are a rough and tumble, sensitive collaborative team; Evidarians living off-planet and hip-hopping through galaxies in a crazily casual way. When on Earth they take on the personas of Matthew Jose (Professor) and Candice James (Sensei).

They are true seekers and gatherers of obscure thoughts and bizarre moments in the quantum boiling pot of timeless time. When they are not writing poetry, their hobby is chasing nuclear butterflies with their collapsible net of poetry as they time travel through their air stream of ink and words, polishing their poems to a super-fine gloss and shine.

If you watch closely you may be able to see them flashing in and out of time on retrograde Moon rotational nights.

Mebbee ... Mebbee not.

www.ingramcontent.com/pod-product-compliance
Lightning Source LLC
Chambersburg PA
CBHW070050120526
44589CB00034B/1784